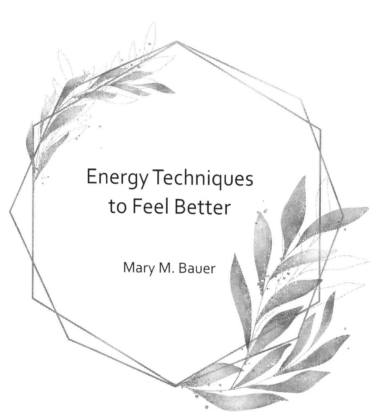

Energy Techniques
to Feel Better

Mary M. Bauer

Cover art: Pixabay

Author photograph: eyelovephoto.com

Cover design and page layout: coversbykaren.com

ISBN: 978-0-9990475-6-9

ALSO BY MARY M. BAUER

40 Conversations with Your Soul ~ A guided journey into self-love

Guarding Clare: A Ransom Mayes Novel

A Clear Understanding of the Unthinkable: What Those Who Died by Suicide Want You to Know (with Kristine Kieland)

For my grandchildren—Jonathon, Ollie, Adeline, Harry, Willie. The wisdom keepers of tomorrow.

And for my incredible Healing Touch mentors—Sarah Stinson, L.P.C., L.P.C.C., CHTP, CHTI and Barb Schommer, RN, MS, CHTP, CHTI.

CONTENTS

Energy Techniques to Feel Better

INTRODUCTION

I had a whole different introduction written for this book—one that backed up energy work with scientific evidence and fact, and I deleted all of it.

I love science. I love proof. But I didn't write this book to convince you of anything. It exists because of my desire to share information and techniques that I think can help you feel better and more in alignment with your inner wisdom by using your own unique life force energy.

You did not create energy (life force), yet you are energy. *Everything*, whether seen or unseen, is energy as Einstein proved over a century ago with his Special Theory of Relativity.

The electromagnetic force field is real and you are part of it. As an electromagnetic energy being, you have control over how you use your life force energy. You do this through your thoughts and feelings.

Your thoughts and feelings give direction to how the massive life force energy co-creates with you. You are forever attracting to yourself circumstances and experiences that are vibrating at the same frequency as you are.

The simplest way I can explain how this works is by using the example (though imperfect) of electricity. You didn't invent electricity, yet you are free to use electricity as you wish by plugging something into an outlet. The electricity doesn't care what you plug into the outlet, or for that matter if you use it at all. And it doesn't care if someone else plugs into it. It works exactly the same for everyone 24/7 without preference or judgement. How it's used is up to you.

So, let's say you want to vacuum the carpet, but plug in a scissors instead of the vacuum cleaner. What do you think will happen? You'll get a shock, right?

Electricity doesn't decide what to plug into the outlet, you do. You can plug in the scissors a thousand times and will get the same result. Electricity won't stop you or change the way it works no matter how many times you hurt yourself. And it doesn't care how badly you want to vacuum the carpet, either. Electricity is cooperating exactly as you determine without judging your desires or actions.

Let's say you begin to realize it hurts a lot when you plug in the scissors, so you try plugging in a coffee maker. Ok, that's some better. At least you're no longer getting painful shocks, but it's still not getting the carpet cleaned.

Ah, now you try plugging in a vacuum cleaner, and yippee! Success! Again, your choice. Electricity simply and awesomely provides the energy needed to use as you determine.

This is a bit the way life force energy works. Your thoughts and feelings are either the scissors, the coffee machine, or the vacuum cleaner. Energy is simply energy and supports your creative endeavors 24/7. You decide whether you're enjoying the experience and the outcome you've created.

If not, it's up to you to change your thoughts and the way you feel about your creation (experience). Determine what thoughts and feelings you need to have in order to be in alignment with what you want to create and think of nothing else.

You are evolving within your own self-created force field. The force field unique to you is called your *aura*. The aura structure is a bit like nesting dolls with layers of subtle vibrations known as energy bodies. Within the energy bodies are multiple energy centers commonly referred to as *chakras*.

But this means nothing if you can't sense or experience the life force within you. If you aren't aware of what your thoughts and emotions are creating, it's hard to believe you are the co-creator of your reality. It's hard to fathom that life is always happening from you, through you, for you as determined by the meaning you give it.

The techniques in this book are designed to help you get in touch with your specific life force energy through an experience that is uniquely yours. ***Use the QR codes for a video demonstration of many of the techniques.***

I've taught these energy techniques in my private client practice, public events and retreats, and I personally use them for my own sense of well-being. The results are reliable, repeatable, and an easy way to relieve whatever stressors, confusions, and misunderstandings you have about your body, your circumstances, and your creative powers.

But proof comes from experience. After using these energy techniques, if you feel better, lighter, calmer, and more enthusiastic about your life, then this little book will have done its job.

BREATHWORK FOR ENERGY, RELAXATION, CREATION

There's a reason breathwork is so popular—it's an intentional technique that brings more oxygen into your body creating balance and calm. A calm, stress free body automatically soothes your mind giving it a new focus of well-being. Problems don't feel quite as insurmountable when you're calm.

Breathwork isn't new. It's been around for thousands of years. Some measurable benefits of breathwork include balanced blood pressure, a release of stress hormones which creates a better immune system, a reduction of anxiety and depression, decrease in addictive behaviors, a longer lasting feeling of well-being, better mental focus and more time in deep sleep. It also gives you a reliable, easy way to calm down providing the self-confidence you need when facing challenges.

TECHNIQUES:

Breathing for Sleep

Nothing feels right if you're not getting the amount of sleep you need to fully rejuvenate and restore the body. Sleep deprivation impairs judgment, stunts memory, kills sex drive, can lead to depression, and contribute to poor health.

Besides physical reasons, there can be many mental/emotional causes for why you may not be getting the rest you need such as worry, inability to shut off your thoughts, depression, anxiety, and so on.

This breathing technique works with your mind giving it something to do, while flooding your body with oxygen which decreases toxins and increases serotonin levels (the feel-good hormone).

The steps:

1. Lie down and get comfy

2. Take a couple deep cleansing breaths to relax.

3. Then begin a repetitious process of inhaling deeply to a slow count of 4, and exhaling completely to a slow count of 7.

4. Inhale for the slow count of 4

5. Exhale for the slow count of 7

6. Continue until sleeping. Usually within 5-10 repetitions.

Counting is not a new concept for sleep, but the odd count fully engages your mind keeping it on task. It has to pay attention to keep its count. It doesn't have time to think of anything else. The additional oxygen flooding your body produces feel-good hormones for relaxation, and removes toxins that keep it in fight or flight mode.

Sweet dreams!

NOTE: If you're having trouble sleeping because of nightmares, or you wake and don't feel rested, try saying this mantra *before* drifting off for the night:

"Nothing can enter my energy field except pure conscious Love."

You are responsible for what you allow into your energy field whether you are awake or sleeping. This simple, direct statement makes it clear that you are 100 percent aware and responsible for your energy. Nothing can broach your field or bother you as long as you consciously say NO. You have total say over your own life force energy.

Palms Up/Palms Down for Receiving and Grounding

When breathing and your palms are up, you're actively receiving. When your palms are down, you're grounding and connecting into your body.

This practice begins by noticing which hand position feels best for what you need right now. Through your experience, you'll know which position to adopt for continuing the breathwork.

The steps:

1. Sit comfortably on a chair or the floor.

2. Place your hands in your lap, palms up. Take a deep breath.

3. Now turn your palms down. Take a deep breath.

4. Turn your palms up. Take a deep breath.

What did you notice? Depending on how your hands were turned, was there a difference in your breathing? Which way did you feel the best?

Now, continue to practice this deep, intentional breathing where your focus is on the breath and the way the body absorbs the breath. Allow your palms to face up if you want to feel more energy or receive from your Highest Wisdom.

Breathe with your palms facing down if you're feeling ungrounded or unsafe, or your thinking feels scattered. This will help you connect with your body and the energies of the earth.

Palms Up/Palms Down for Receiving and Grounding
https://youtu.be/AmCNZKHVUNA (1:26)

6-Minute Gratitude Meditation

This powerful technique can help you tap into your inner guidance and feel secure in all the good you've already created in your life. By using gratitude to align with what you already know to be true for you, you can stay in this high-vibe energy flow as you concentrate on what you want most in your future.

This is an intense active meditation that requires open-mouth breathing—two inhales to one exhale. (The QR code demonstrates the breathwork required.)

This system inundates the body with oxygen and endorphins, relaxing the nervous system. Bringing in all that oxygen can create physical sensations such as feelings of cold, hot, tingly, floating, heaviness, tightness, light-headedness, numbness, waves of emotions, tears, memories. Or you might not know what you're feeling. These are all ways to process what's held within your cells and energy field.

Use this breathing meditation to release your body from trauma, cultivate gratitude, and create the life you most want to live.

The steps:

1. Lie down, get comfy, close your eyes, arms at side, legs uncrossed.

2. Begin the active open-mouth breath. With your mouth open, inhale into your solar plexus (belly), inhale into your heart, then exhale through your mouth. Take two inhales to one exhale.

3. For two minutes, focus on everything in your life that you're grateful for.

4. Good! Continue the active breath. For the next two minutes, focus on everything you're grateful for today, including specific people in your life and specific circumstances that you now see as a benefit.

5. Continue the active breath. During the last two minutes, focus on everything you're grateful for that you're creating in your future.

6. When finished, come back to your regular breath (one inhale, one exhale). Continue to rest and breathe normally. Sit up slowly. Drink at least one glass of water.

You can speed up or slow down your breath. Do what feels right for you. You can also extend the time you spend in gratitude and deep breathing. Start by adding on another three minutes, and so on.

6-Minute Gratitude Meditation
https://youtu.be/uLKaVuw3Lu8 (1:21)

When you're excited about something, it feels like you're soaring with energy. When you're sad or depressed, you might have no energy at all and have a difficult time motivating yourself. If you feel anxious, it's often hard to stop worrying or thinking about a problem. Emotions change your energy vibration.

This easy technique will help you stay balanced and build your vibration when you're feeling unsettled, emotional, or scattered in your thinking.

The steps:

1. Sit on the floor or in a chair. Relax and get comfy. Close your eyes. As you inhale deeply through your nose, visualize all your energy coming back to you as sparkling bright light.

2. Exhale a short, powerful burst out through your mouth, and as you do, visualize any energy you're holding that isn't yours or no longer serves you, released back to the Universe as sparkling bright light. (Trust that the Universe knows exactly what to do with this energy.)

3. Repeat three times, or as often as feels good to you.

Notice how you feel. Does it feel as if your shoulders are lighter, like a weight has been lifted? Is your mind clearer, your emotions calmer?

Take Back Your Energy
https://youtu.be/Bdzhe3FVAYM (1:22)

CHAKRA ALIGNMENT

Chakra (pronounced *chuhk rah*) is an ancient Sanskrit word that refers to the spinning disks of energy in your body. These energy centers correspond to specific bundles of nerves, major organs, and the energy bodies that affect your physical, emotional, mental, and spiritual well-being.

Your body has many energy centers, but we're going to concentrate on the alignment of the major chakras that run from the base of your spine to center top of your head. The techniques in this chapter help balance and maintain these chakras for optimum health and vitality.

NOTE: Here's a little information about the chakras, their locations up the center of the body, the colors associated with each, and the energy they embody:

- **Root (or Base):** located near the tailbone, color red—stability, bravery, courage, grounded, strength, determination, security

- **Sacral:** located roughly two inches below the navel, color orange—harmony, spontaneity, creativity, passion, physical vitality, emotions, sacred sensuality and sexuality

- **Solar Plexus:** located about two inches above the navel, color yellow—intelligence, confidence, personal power, independence, individuality, flexibility, personality, humor, Divine will

- **Heart:** located center of chest across from physical heart, color green—joy, faith, compassion, miracles, magic

- **High Heart** (thymus): located 1.5 inches above the heart center, color pink or aqua—selfless devotion to Universal creation, unconditional love, joy

- **Throat:** located center of throat, color sky blue—language, communication, magnetism, truth, honesty

- **Brow (or Third Eye):** located center of forehead about 1.5 inches above eyebrows, color cobalt blue—psychic vision, clairvoyance, intuition, crystal clear clarity

- **Crown:** located center top of head, color purple—Divine wisdom, Divine connection, ascended mastery, ecstasy, bliss, humbleness, illumination

- **Transpersonal Point:** located twelve inches above center of head in the auric field, color white or gold—Christ consciousness, connection to God Self

TECHNIQUES:

Headache Reliever

When stress or tension build in the energy system, sometimes the result is a nasty headache. Here's a few energy techniques that help alleviate headache pain.

Technique 1:

1. Lay the palm of your hand over your forehead (brow chakra).

2. Lay the palm of your other hand over the base of your skull where it connects with your spine.

3. Hold the position and relax as you take some deep breaths

4. You may feel warmth or tingles in your palms or head. Hold position until you feel better.

Technique 2:

1. Lay the palm of your hand over your forehead (brow chakra).

2. Lay the palm of your other hand at the back of your head directly across from your forehead.

3. Hold the position and relax as you deep breathe.

   a. You may feel warmth, tingles, or a pulsing feeling between your hands. Hold the position until the pain releases. The energy goes straight through your head.

NOTE: You can also keep your hand on your forehead (brow chakra) and place the other hand on top of your head. Follow the same instructions until you get relief.

Technique 3:

   a. If you're having a temple headache, place your fingertips on your temples and apply a bit of gentle pressure (or whatever feels comfortable for you).

   b. Take a nice deep breath, close your eyes. The tips of your fingers act like energy lasers and will begin to pulse back and forth placing the energy where you need it most.

   c. Hold the position until the pain subsides.

   d. Play around with the different hand positions until you find what works best for you.

Headache Reliever
https://youtu.be/rYUsCGtfPVo (2:59)

Head Pump

A simple technique that does the work of a mini craniosacral massage by promoting the flow of synovial fluid and energy through your spine, releasing tension and pain throughout the body. Use this powerful exercise whenever you're feeling tired, brain fog, in pain, or like the weight of the world is on your shoulders.

The steps:

1. Place your fingers at the base of your skull and apply gentle pressure.

2. Pump (nod) your head up and down 10 times until you feel better.

Notice how your body feels afterward. Does it feel lighter? Tingly? Warm? Less fatigued? Maybe you felt a vibration move through your entire body and now there's less pain or you can think [1]with more clarity?

Head Pump
https://youtu.be/ox9idaQUpC8 (1:17)

Physical Chakra Alignment Exercise

Your body is the ultimate sensing device and often stores unresolved emotions as tensions or pain in your tissues, cells, organs, nerves, and energy fields. This simple exercise helps release these tensions and opens your chakras for optimum energy and ease.

The steps:

1. Sit comfortably, or lie down, legs uncrossed. Close your eyes.

    a. Take 3 deep breaths, and relax.

2. Now, bring your focus to your feet. Tense your feet, only your feet as best you can for a slow count of 10.

    a. Take a deep breath, and relax your feet.

3. Bring your attention to the calves of your legs. Tense your calves, only your calves as best you can for a slow count of 10.

    a. Take a deep breath, and relax your calves.

4. Tense only your thighs for a slow count of 10.

    a. Take a deep breath, and relax.

5. Tense only your hips, buttocks, and stomach muscles for a slow count of 10.

    a. Take a deep breath, and relax

6. Tense only your chest, shoulders, back, and arms for a slow count of 10. Make a fist to help you tense the area.

    a. Take a deep breath, and relax.

7. Tense only your face, neck, and back of your head for a slow count of 10. Make a face to help you tense the area.

   a. Take a deep breath, and relax.

8. Take one more deep breath, wiggle your fingers and toes. Open your eyes, fully relaxed.

What do you notice? Does your body feel tingly, more relaxed? Are your tensions lessened? Do you feel lighter, your body more connected? Do you have more clarity?

You can do this exercise anytime you don't feel good and positive about yourself or the world in general. It helps clear all your chakras with minimum effort. It's also a great way to relax before sleep.

Physical Chakra Alignment Exercise
https://youtu.be/5j-1zp3lBPY (6:04)

Push In, Pull Up

If you're feeling scattered or just plain "off," this simple technique quickly aligns and strengthens your energy centers by supporting your nervous system, reducing anxiety, and clearing your mind.

The steps:

a. Place the middle finger of one hand inside your navel, and place the middle finger of your other hand at the center of your forehead about an inch above your eyebrows

a. Push in and pull up.

a. Breathe deeply and slowly several times, or until you feel better. Your eyes can be open or closed, whatever feels right for you.

Push In, Pull Up
https://youtu.be/CoLsnOjBo44 (1:28)

Raking Through Your Energy Field

There are many subtle energy bodies that make up your biofield (life force energy), commonly referred to as your aura. Your physical body is housed within your biofield. You've probably had a sense of your biofield when someone stood a little too close to you. It felt like they were in your space, right? That's because they were standing in your biofield.

When you're healthy and feel good about yourself and the world around you, your biofield extends about two feet from your body in a nice egg shape.

When you're suffering mentally, emotionally, physically, or spiritually, your biofield becomes misshapen and the energy centers (chakras) don't work like they should. It's important to keep a nice strong energy field to help your body stay healthy and your life balanced.

The steps:

1. Begin this exercise by imagining the ends of your fingertips are like magnets. You're going to use your fingers like magnets as you rake through your energy field pulling out anything that isn't helpful.

2. Set the intention that anything you no longer need in your field, or anything that isn't serving your highest good, is released with ease and grace.

3. Begin with your hands about a foot above your head and rake downward over your body without touching it. Imagine the magnets at the ends of your fingers picking up all the debris in your energy field.

4. As you rake through your field, pay attention to the sensations you're picking up through your hands. Maybe they feel warm, or cold, or wet, or tingly, or prickly, or achy, or sticky. Maybe you don't feel anything. There's no wrong way to feel.

5. Repeat the process until you have a sense that your field is "clean," or smoother. You may feel lighter, less fatigued, or your hands might feel calmer with a smoother vibration running through them.

6. Then soothe your energy field by using smoothing hand motions, almost like you're petting a cat.

If your child is having an off day or not feeling the best, you can rake through their field as well. It generally takes less time to rake through a child's field, but the steps are the same.

Your pet also has an energy field and can benefit from this technique, but never rake through anyone's field (including your pet) without first getting their permission. You'll know if your pet doesn't want this kind of help because you'll feel shocks in your hands and most likely they'll snarl or snap at you.

Raking Through Your Energy Field
https://youtu.be/kodIsmZ-xkc (2:42)

Sun Chakra Energy Boost

The sun's rays not only help your body produce Vitamin D, it also feeds your chakras with powerful light energy. Here's a simple way to raise your vibration and reduce stress by connecting with sun energy.

The steps:

1. Go outside, close your eyes and lift your face to the sun.

2. Place your hand over your heart, and take several slow, deep breaths.

3. Keep your eyes closed and as you breathe, you'll begin to notice an array of neon colors. Bright colors: red, orange, yellow, green, blue, cobalt blue, purple, gold, white. These are the colors of your energy centers (chakras).

4. Breathe in these colors as they appear and you'll start to feel better.

As you breathe through this technique, don't judge what comes. You'll see the colors you most need. If you can't see anything, activities like walking help open your field. Alternate between walking and facing the sun. What did you notice as you brought in your colors? How did your body feel? Did you receive insights?

GROUNDING INTO YOUR ENERGY BODIES

The term "grounding" as this book uses it, means getting in touch with, and centering into, your peaceful authentic nature through the use of techniques that help you refocus your attention from thoughts and worries to the present moment where life is actually lived.

Grounding into your energy bodies refers to your personal biofield (aura) that extends about two feet around your physical body. These are subtle energies that can be sensed. Think about when someone stands too close to you. It feels like they're in your space, right? They are standing in your biofield which contains at least seven subtle energy bodies— etheric, emotional, mental, astral, etheric template, celestial, and ketheric template.

Your biofield energizes your physical body and also creates your perception of reality. Grounding into your energy bodies assures that you are tapped into your personal electromagnetic energy field for optimum clarity, wisdom, health, and well-being.

Note: As you shift your energy into your highest vibration, it's a good idea to ask everything in your personal environment to shift with you. This is easily accomplished by your intention. Just ask that all your appliances, technologies, electronics, garage door opener, and all devices in your home shift into the new frequency with you. This assures that all your devices and appliances don't suddenly and mysteriously break down because of the higher electromagnetic frequency you are now holding within your energy field.

TECHNIQUES:

Body Blueprint Repatterning

Your energy field is the blueprint for your physical body. The body will create what the blueprint dictates.

This meditative visualization technique is used to restore and revitalize the seven subtle energy bodies of the biofield (auric blueprint). These are the etheric, emotional, mental, astral, etheric template, celestial, ketheric template.

Through different prompts, you'll work within your auric field to identify any and all disruptive patterns (or anything that seems "off"), and use your own best way to correct and create new patterns of wholeness. *Trust that you know your best way to heal your own unique energy field.*

Body Blueprint Repatterning is helpful in relieving chronic pain, anxiety, depression, malaise, self-doubt, feelings of unworthiness and ineffectiveness. It also helps boost the immune system, and gives relief from any type of surgical pain or injury. This method can bring a sense of control if you're feeling out of control.

The steps *before* beginning Body Blueprint Repatterning:

1. Think of something you're struggling with. Maybe you have pain somewhere in your body, or anxiety over a circumstance? Maybe you're feeling some sadness, or grief? Or whatever it is you're feeling whether it's an emotion or pain, give it a rating between 1 and 10. Number 1 is the least severe, 10 the most severe.

2. Now put your phone on silent so you won't be disturbed for at least 30 minutes.

3. Dim the lights, then lie down and get comfy.

4. When ready, que the technique through the QR code, then close your eyes.

Remember, as you listen to the guided meditation, you are in control at all times and may end the session at any time. You will do all the work to make the changes and connections within your body. You are always in charge.

Afterward: recheck your number. What is it now? Is your pain or emotion less severe? Maybe it's gone? You can do this technique whenever you're in pain or overly emotional, feel stuck, or your life feels out of control.

Body Blueprint Repatterning
https://youtu.be/QyiAzCG9zS4 (23:13)

Feeling Your Energy

Even though science has proven the energy field exists, it most likely remains a concept until you experience it for yourself. Experience is what makes it real.

This technique helps you have a tangible experience of sensing your own unique energy field. It also helps relieve stress, pain, and is a great way to self-soothe.

The steps:

1. Vigorously rub the palms of your hands together for about a minute. Slowly pull your hands apart about 4-6 inches. What do you notice? Warmth? Tingling? Maybe a little vibration of some kind? This is your energy. It's okay if you don't sense anything, just imagine that you can.

2. Keep your hands in place and build on this energy by taking a deep breath, and then another. Relax completely.

3. Now imagine a golden ray of sunshine entering the top of your head, going down through the center of your head, down through your neck, out into your shoulders, your arms, and into the palms of your hands.

4. Breathe deeply and bring in as much of this golden light as you can. Feel the energy in your hands. How does it feel? Is there pressure? Warmth? Are they pulsing?

5. Keep breathing and visualizing this energy building between your palms, getting larger. Smile. Notice how your smile increases the energy.

6. With both hands, cover your heart. This brings your loving, beautiful energy into your heart.

7. Take a deep breath and relax, absorbing your own life-affirming energy. Imagine this energy going through your whole body. This is conscious recognition of your authentic nature moving through your body.

As another option, instead of bringing the energy into your heart, you can put the energy wherever you need it most, like your belly, your head, or any place you have pain. Listen to your body and it will tell you where it needs the energy.

Feeling Your Energy
https://youtu.be/YkQY-dehP7Y (4:56)

Be a Tree Technique

There are many ways to enhance your spiritual connection so you feel grounded in your body. Meditation, yoga, music, etc. *Be a Tree* is a fun, yet powerful way to stay physically centered within your body while consciously connecting with your highest Source energy.

Do this exercise when you feel scattered, down, in doubt, low self-esteem, exhausted, or want more energy.

The steps:

1. Stand tall and sturdy with your feet flat on the ground and about 18 inches apart. Stretch your arms up past your head, hands flat and open, fingers pointing skyward.

2. Now close your eyes and imagine yourself as a tree. Imagine how your roots feel absorbing the earth's pure fresh water, the minerals you need from the soil, and all that beautiful earth energy you need to grow and maintain your amazing body.

3. Imagine all this good stuff coming up through your body, the trunk of your being. Imagine what this pure, vital energy would feel like. Do you feel anything? What do you suppose it would feel like to bring up all the minerals and water and energy from the earth into your feet and flowing upward into your trunk, into your branches (arms) and through your leaves (hands)?

4. Now imagine shining all this good energy out your leaves as a gift to the sun, because the sun doesn't know the earth in quite the same way you do. Imagine and invite the sun to come into your leaves and into

your body with its healing warmth, filling you up with its energy. What would that feel like?

5. Then send this healing energy out through your roots into the rich soil as you become the bridge between the sun and the earth, between your heavenly spiritual essence and your physical form. What does that feel like?

Continue flowing the energy from the earth, through your body and outward into the heavens, then pull that energy downward into your body and send it into the earth. This is a beautiful and easy grounding technique that will fill you with energy and calming peace.

Tip the Tail Grounding

Nothing quite centers you into your body like the Tip the Tail technique. You're creating a bit of gentle tension from your waist through your hips and downward into your legs and feet. This engages and opens three of your major chakras—solar plexus, sacral, and root which play a role in the way you view yourself in the world.

A great technique if you feel unsafe, overly emotional, lack confidence, or need to get the creative juices flowing.

The steps:

1. Stand with your feet parallel 18-24 inches apart, toes pointing forward.

2. Slightly bend your knees

3. Tip your pelvis in and forward, pull stomach in

4. Create tension from your waist down, as if you're trying to push your knees together but maintain their distance

5. Hold position for a slow count of 20

If you want to connect your entire chakra system at the same time, hold your position and place one hand on your heart, and the other on the top of your head. Breathe deep and slow as you count to 20.

Tip the Tail Grounding
https://youtu.be/9kKtsOYE2al (3:09)

JOURNAL THERAPY

Journaling is a form of writing therapy that focuses on your internal experiences through your thoughts and feelings in order to gain clarity and a deeper understanding of yourself. This practical tool is great for letting go of intense emotions that can harm your body, your relationships, your career and more if not understood and released.

Use your journal to vent frustrations, work out problems, ask questions and receive answers from your highest, wisest Self. The answers often range from profound to practical and are always helpful.

The reason journaling is included in this energy book is because it's another way to help you get in touch with your highest Source frequency—the one Source that is uniquely yours, loves you like no one else, and holds nothing but your highest good at all times. It sees what you can't sometimes, which is your bigger picture, and will deliver your messages with kindness, compassion, and love. Once you receive your answers or work out your problems, you feel better and your whole energy field shifts into something more authentically you.

You can get started journaling by writing down what you feel, or an experience you need clarity about, or simply ask your questions. With a little patience, your answers will come. You'll know they are right because they're helpful and you'll feel good about yourself.

TECHNIQUES:

Empty Your Heart Space

Did you know you have a soul message center inside your body? You do. It's your heart. Love and joy flow directly through your heart as high vibe inspiration, peace, and well-being.

Take a look at your heart. What kind of shape is it in? Does your heart feel heavy? Burdened? Angry? Grief-stricken? Is your heart inbox so stuffed with stagnant emotions and bitter memories that there's no room for mail from your soul? Are you missing out on your most important life-affirming messages? If so, journaling is a quick way to declutter your heart inbox.

The steps:

1. Write down everything that comes to your mind. Write all your pain, all your hatreds, all your dreams, all your goals, all your unworthiness, guilt, doubt, fears. Write all your regrets, jealousies, worries, sorrows, traumas.

2. Write as fast as you can without judgement for what comes.

3. Don't read anything. Just write, and let everything pour from you. Your heart knows what needs to be released.

4. Then immediately tear up your pages and burn everything. Set the intention that all your released thoughts and emotions convert to sparkly creative energy.

And that's all there is to it. Write. Burn. Write. Burn. Write. Burn. But absolutely NO judging or reading.

You may have to empty your heart ten times, or one hundred times, or one thousand times, or more. But the day will come when your heart feels light, spacious, full of love and appreciation for everything in your life. That's when you know your heart inbox is open and ready to receive your soul messages.

Self-rejection is the most painful thing you'll ever do to yourself.

There are many ways you actively participate in self-rejection without consciously realizing you're doing it. One way is when you listen to your cruel inner critic who constantly undermines your self-worth. Another is believing someone's viewpoint has more authority than your own inner guidance.

And another huge way is every time you say "yes" to someone or some project when you really mean "no," *is self-rejection*. You're making someone else's wishes more important than your own stellar inner guidance. There's a reason you don't want to do something. Trust it. Own it. Decide *for* you and not against.

Going against what you know to be true for you is incredibly painful as you have to force yourself to be okay with something you don't want to do. You might think it's no big deal to do this, but it sets up conflict within. Remember the introduction at the beginning of this book? Going against yourself is the same thing as you willingly plugging a scissors into an outlet. You're going to get hurt.

Now you know you're a responsible person. You're not going to stop paying your bills or taking care of your loved ones. That's not what self-rejection is about. Self-rejection is when you agree to do a fundraiser you don't want to do, go to a luncheon or meeting you don't want to attend, push yourself to finish a project when your body says rest.

Self-rejection is also when you want to do something, are enthusiastic about it, but talk yourself out of it with excuses like: I don't have the money, don't have the time, don't have the experience, don't have the courage, don't need it, I'm not good enough.

Sound familiar? While some of your excuses may be valid, also know you wouldn't have had the desire if it wasn't a possibility for you. The Universal energy always says yes to every one of your thoughts and feelings. What are you telling it to help you create? More of what you want or more of what you don't want? You attract what you focus on.

So, get out your journal. Here's a simple, yet profound first step for creating your best life by identifying and eliminating what you don't want to do which frees up room in your life for the things more in alignment with your heart's desires.

The steps:

1. List all the things you love to do. Get detailed here. Nothing is too small or insignificant to list. If you love to do it, list it.

2. Now list all the things you're doing because you feel you *should*. Get detailed. Nothing is too small or insignificant. If you are doing something out of obligation or guilt, list it.

3. List all the things you'd like to do more of. Get detailed.

4. List all the things you'd like to do because they make you feel good, but you're currently not doing them. These can be simple things and big things. Your bucket list can be part of this. Let yourself really dream.

5. Look your lists over. Which is longer?

6. How would you feel if you crossed all the "shoulds" off your list?

7. Pick two items on the "should" list and cross them off. What action will you take to fully eliminate them? Can you pick two more? Can you eventually cross all the items off the list and not add any more things to it?

You can't have the life you want doing the things you want if you've filled every moment with things you don't want. Every time you need to make a decision, ask yourself, *does this feel like something I get to do, or something I should do?* Your Soul purpose feels like something you get to do, and sometimes it feels like a burning desire. You put yourself in conflict when you ignore your guidance.

Some simple, but honest ways to say no:

•   Thank you for thinking of me, but it's a pass this time. I'm taking a little break for some me-time.

•   Thank you for thinking of me, but I'm working on listening to myself and not taking on more projects than what feels right and balanced for me.

•   Thank you for thinking of me, but I'm not the right person for this job/position/project.

•   Thank you for thinking of me, but no thank you.

Trust your heart whispers. Say what you mean right away. Don't go against yourself and you'll create your best life.

SOUND ALIGNMENT

Sound healing has been around forever. If you've ever shifted your mood by listening to a favorite song, then you've experienced a sound healing. There are many. From toning, to the Solfeggio frequencies, to drumming, Tibetan and crystal bowls, tuning forks, nature sounds, and more, sound therapy is a viable way to restore balance to your energy field through vibration.

The sound techniques in this book are strictly voice-activated in order to clear and align your energy field.

TECHNIQUES:

AUM Mantra

Your tongue mixes sound in complex ways forming language, but there are three basic universal sounds that even a tongue isn't needed in order to create them. These basic sounds are: ah, ooh, mm.

The sound AUM (ahh---ooo—mmm) is used to stimulate and balance the mental, emotional, and physical energy bodies. This technique is useful for attention disorders, a healthy body, speaking up, and if you're having excessive fear or nightmares.

Here's a few things you should know before beginning the AUM mantra:

The first sound Ahh is accomplished with an open mouth. As you begin to slowly close your mouth, you'll naturally expel the sound Ooo without changing anything except the closing of your lower jaw. The sound Mmm is created when your mouth is completely closed.

As you naturally produce each sound, bring your attention to where you feel the sound vibration in your body.

Ahh is the point located about an inch below the naval and takes the energy vibration right across the body. This sound strengthens your entire energy system.

Ooo starts just below the rib cage. Vibrations go down, then up and around the creative/heart center.

Mmm starts at the pit of the throat and spreads upward in the body to the tip of your nose.

The steps:

1. To begin, sit with your left foot pressed against your perineum. This is for a sense of security and grounding within. Also, in this position your body functions decrease, and the urge to eat and go to the bathroom lessen.

2. Bring your right foot in front of left

3. Now hold the Yoga Mudra where your thumb and index finger (of both hands) touch creating a circle, the other fingers are together in a straight line. Place hands on thighs, arms loose, comfortable. Only the tips of your fingers to the wrist should have a bit of tension in them.

4. Practice by first expressing each sound separately. Make the sound Ahh in one breath for as long as you can. Repeat 7X

5. Close your jaw halfway without any change to tongue position, lips, or anything else. Make the sound Ooo in one breath for as long as you can. Repeat 7X.

6. Close your mouth without making any changes and make the sound Mmm for as long as you can. Repeat 7X,

7. Now put the sounds together in one long breath for as long as you can, changing only your jaw position. This produces the natural sound of AUM. The goal is to roughly create the same amount of time between sounds. Do this 21X

8. Journal your experience.

As you utter AUM, notice the vibrations in your body move from your navel to the tip of your nose. Watch and feel your energy moving through your body. This is an active meditation, not an unconscious repetition. Stay actively aware of how your body feels as you utter each sound. Practice on a daily basis for a clear, robust energy field.

AUM Mantra
https://youtu.be/4LD--PfYe-M (13:14)

Say Your Name

Throughout the day, there are so many distractions vying for your attention such as problems, loved ones, to-do lists, other people, pets, social media, memories, thoughts of the future, and daily living. This type of distractive thinking/ feeling/doing is often done without conscious awareness. It seems sort of natural, yet it will leave you feeling drained and scattered.

Why? Because thought is energy and when we're absently thinking/feeling/doing on auto-pilot without edit, we're giving our life force to distractions that scatter and weaken our energy field. In other words, we've given a little of our energy everywhere to lots of things. We're not fully present in our body. We've created a few gaps, holes, and blocks in our energy system, and we feel it as brain fog and exhaustion. The solution is simple. Call your energy back to you.

The steps:

1. Close your eyes, take a deep breath.

2. Say your name out loud three times. Use the name you resonate with most. When you say your name out loud, you're consciously connecting with the signature energy that is yours during your lifetime.

As you do this technique, pay attention to your heart area. You'll feel a subtle movement or click during one of the times you call your name. Or you might feel a movement through your shoulder or neck instead of your heart. Everyone's experience is unique to them.

If you don't feel anything, call your name three times again. Try using your full birth name, or your married name, or a nickname. The movement is subtle, but after this exercise you'll feel lighter and more like yourself again.

Say Your Name
https://youtu.be/VX1aKJHM7Zo (2:14)

Scream Out Your Anger

When frustration and anger build in our bodies without release, the energy gets trapped in our liver. In ancient times, the Chinese found that by using the primal scream the blocked emotions released, and the body came back into balance. They discovered yelling was good for the lungs and the liver.

Primal scream was popularized as Scream Therapy in the 1970's. It was used as a way to relieve tension, stress, anger, frustration, anxiety, pain, depression, overwhelm, and self-doubt. New research shows that it also increases strength and stabilizes your core. That's why you'll notice people at the gym give a little grunt or yell before strenuous exercise, and tennis players let go with a loud grunt as they hit the ball. It gives them added stability and strength.

When anger and frustration build in a person, it usually equals a blow up at someone close to them—children, spouse, partner, pet, neighbor, sibling, co-worker, boss, etc.

Anger is a big emotion. It holds a ton of space in your body and is a huge force when expelled. It comes out like a runaway train and will level everything in its track. Afterward, the person doing the yelling feels pretty good, but the other person is traumatized because the human scream activates a fear response deep in the mind of the person getting yelled at.

If you feel anger or any other big emotion building inside you, it's time to open up that voice chakra and let off some steam in a harmless way before you end up hurting someone. And while this technique won't get to the core of your emotional issue, it can provide an immediate release so you feel better. Here's some suggestions:

- Scream into a pillow.

- Turn the radio up full volume and sing at the top of your lungs. You don't need the words, just let the sound come out. Loud.

- Once you get into your car after work, scream as loud as you can all the way home (or all the way to work).

- Shout while you exercise.

- Get a screaming buddy and scream together.

- Find a secluded spot in nature and scream.

Scream until the pressure releases and you feel calm and good. Know this is a viable, easy way to be compassionate and loving to yourself, your body, and your loved ones.

STILLING THE MIND

Have you ever put bread in a toaster, pushed down the lever, and nothing happened? No toast. What? Then you realize the toaster isn't even plugged in. This is pretty much what happens when you're not plugged into your life force energy.

Nothing works when you're distracted by pain, anxiety, blame, guilt, regret. You're basically plugged into a story in your head and not your energy. All thoughts are creative. Letting these thoughts run wild without editing creates the opposite of what you want.

But there's lots you can do to change addictive reactionary thinking in favor of a peaceful mind that works for you and not against. These techniques will help.

TECHNIQUES:

Clock Focus

If every moment of every day is filled with thoughts, there's no room for your highest wisdom to come through. This is what's call a mind loop and it'll keep you stuck in the same old thinking. Instead of creating solutions to your problems, you'll feel like your problems are multiplying and insurmountable.

This exercise creates a gap in the mind loop. It teaches you how to take a break from the inner critic by allowing some space in your stream of thought so you receive your highest wisdom. Do this technique when you want peace, a clear mind, creative ideas and solutions.

The steps:

1. You'll need a clock with a second hand.

2. Stare at the second hand. This gives your active mind something to do.

3. Keep your mind blank—no thought, as you watch the seconds tick by. Concentrate only on watching the second hand without thought.

4. If thoughts come up, no worries. Just start over. The goal is 15 seconds without thought.

5. Once you accomplish 15 seconds without thought, extend it to 30 seconds, then 45 seconds and so on until you can do a full two minutes without thought.

Two minutes without thought can change your life. In the absence of incessant thought/thinker/analyzer/critic, there is only pure consciousness—the knower, the absolute wisdom of ALL. This is the space of quiet solution, the aha eureka moments. This is your highest creation vibration.

The technique seems simple, deceptively so at first, because so many thoughts will want to rush in. But keep at it 15 seconds at a time. Keep your mind focused on the second hand of the clock. You are an observer without thought. It will get easier and as it does, you'll notice life feels much more peaceful and your solutions appear faster.

Committed Mindfulness

This is one of the most useful techniques to feel big emotions and neutralize them without blaming, shaming, or building a big story in your mind that keeps you stuck in a non-ending loop. Committed Mindfulness will help you take control of your mind so you are consciously choosing your thoughts and not being lead down a rabbit hole of pain.

This technique encourages you to name the feeling without making a personal story out of it. The reason you name the feeling is to get it out in the open. No denying or stuffing, both hurt the body by elevating stress hormones. Name it, and the body is happy you got its message.

The steps:

1. As soon as you recognize you're having a big feeling, name it by saying it. For example, say: *Anger is present.* NOT I'm angry because this person was mean to me. That's story. Simply state what's true. Anger is present. Or sadness is present. Or whatever feeling is present. Notice how neutral that feels. By calling out the feeling without attaching a story, the feeling is simply there. Neutral. Natural. Your body is happy because you acknowledged what it feels.

2. Your mind will automatically want to loop you into a story. That's the dysfunctional pattern you're ready to end. To prevent the story such as *anger is present because so and so did this horrible thing to me...* immediately use a safe word to take control of your mind. Your safe word can be anything. Banana is a good one. Neutral, easy to visualize. But it can be anything— your dog's name, a favorite food, place, word, etc. Now your mind has something besides story to focus on.

3. Then take a deep breath and instantly commit to something. Committing to drinking a glass of water is good, but anything works. How that looks:

   a. Say out loud (or to yourself if not alone): I'm committing to getting a glass of water. Then go pour yourself a glass of water.

   b. Next say: I'm committed to drinking this glass of water. Then drink the water.

   c. Then say: I'm committed to putting this glass in the dishwasher. Put the glass in the dishwasher, and so on.

4. By consciously choosing something to commit to gives you complete control over what you want your mind to think. You're no longer in a patterned loop. By immediately following through with action, your body now knows it can trust that you'll do what you say. It feels safe and calms down. You can commit to anything physical. Blinking your eyes, jumping on one foot, holding up each of your fingers one at a time, etc.

5. To keep control of your thoughts and prevent your mind from recreating the story loop, have a bucket list going of things you'd like to try or have happen in your life. List at least ten things specifically for you that sound like fun. List big holy cow things and small interesting things. Maybe you'd like to camp on Hawaii with the cowboys, swim with wild dolphins, visit a dark park, name a star, eat a fruit you never tried before. Put the things on your list that feel good to you.

6. When you finish committing to something, think about something on your bucket list. See yourself doing this thing you want. Feel what it's like to do this thing. This

is the way to take control of your thoughts and create a future you want without dragging the old patterns forward.

Be gentle with yourself. Breaking a pattern takes practice, but you will succeed!

Retrain the Brain

Neuroscience has proven that it's absolutely possible to train your brain to look for enough safety, satisfaction, connection, fullness, contentment, appreciation, and love.

In short, you can retrain your brain to focus on your good which creates new neural pathways in your brain that calm and bring more of what you like in your life. Simultaneously, this takes the focus off the old brain patterns that over time can cause mental, emotional and physical imbalances and illness.

By pausing a moment to consciously imprint your brain with your enjoyable experiences, you help the mind/body work for you to break old patterns and create more of what you love.

The steps:

1. To begin retraining your brain, first pay attention to how you feel when you're enjoying something whether it's food, stimulating conversation, a stunning sunrise, flowers in a roadside ditch, a child's laughter, a raise in your pay, a funny joke, the smell of the air after a thunderstorm, the sight of birds in flight, music, or whatever it is that causes you to feel joy.

2. In that joyful moment, close your eyes for a second and take an extra deep breath to slow things down. In that moment become hyper aware of what you're feeling, and consciously stay with that good experience an extra moment.

3. Touch your heart and say to yourself, "*This is my good. This is what I'm looking for. **More please.**"*

4. Feel the good experience within your body. Where do you feel it? How do you sense it? Focus on what's rewarding about it. Keep feeling the sensation in your body for as long as you can.

This simple, enjoyable technique is a favorite, because it works fast and has the potential to totally change your view of your world. Within a week of consistent practice, my clients report feeling much better about themselves and their lives with noticeably less depression, stress, worry, and anxiety. They also report noticing a lot more synchronistic and aha moments. Not a bad tradeoff for a moment's pause.

Beautiful Reader,

Thank you for reading Energy Techniques to Feel Better. These are some of my favorite ways to center and balance. If you enjoyed this book, please consider leaving a rating and review. Your comments really help new books get noticed, and I greatly appreciate every review.

With great love for your journey,

Mary

Mary's contact information:

Website: www.marymbauer.com

Email: marymbauer.author@gmail.com

Sign up for Mary's free weekly newsletter with tips and techniques in support of your mental, emotional, physical, and spiritual journey: http://bit.ly/mary-optin

ABOUT THE AUTHOR

Mary M. Bauer is an energy intuitive, spiritual teacher, and author. She has helped thousands of people heal trauma and create their best lives by using her insight, compassion, love, and energy techniques. In addition to Healing Touch and Reiki, Mary is skilled in a multitude of wellness disciplines.

Through her private practice, books, and workshops, she provides guidance and support for the release of physical, mental, emotional, and spiritual blocks, and is dedicated to helping people understand their unique energy system and conscious use of creative thought. You can learn more about Mary and her work at: www.marymbauer.com

Made in the USA
Middletown, DE
25 August 2024

59089424R00035